A MULE NAMED FRANK

BY
DONNA WEBERNICK

A MULE NAMED FRANK

BY

DONNA WEBERNICK

ALL GRAPHICS WERE
TAKEN FROM CANVA AND MADE INTO MY DESIGN

Dear Reader,

I hope you enjoy reading my book "A Mule Named Frank." Thank you for your purchase.

Many blessings,

Donna Webernick

Farmer Joe needed a mule for his farm, so he went to Mr. Bill, who had one for sale.

Farmer Joe drove his truck and trailer to the farm to buy a mule.

Upon his arrival at the farm, he was welcomed by Mr. Bill.

Mr. Bill said to Farmer Joe, "Pick anyone from this field."

So, Joe found the one he wanted, paid for him, and loaded him onto the trailer to go home.

When Joe arrived home, his wife came to see the
mule he had purchased.

She laughed and asked, "What will you name him?"

He said to his wife, "I'm going to name him Frank."
She chuckled.

"Welcome to your new home, Frank," the wife said.

Farmer Joe placed Frank in the field to graze for the time being.

Joe's children came home from school and were surprised to see a new animal in the pasture. They asked their dad, "What is the mule's name?" Dad replied, "His name is Frank."

The children invited the neighbors' kids to see Frank.

One of the children brought Frank a basket of apples for him to eat.

Frank adores his apples; he devoured each one until none remained.

Betty wanted to ride on Frank; he just loved the attention he was getting from the children.

As the day passed, the children took turns riding Frank individually.

When it was time for the children to leave, they said "goodbye" to Frank and their friends.

Farmer Joe removed Frank's saddle so that he could rest.

He then took Frank to the barn to give him some hay.

Joe said to his wife, "What a fun day for Frank and the children."

She replied, "And for you, too."

Farmer Joe told his wife, "I'm hungry and ready for bed."

She told Joe, "The children have eaten and have gone to bed."

Joe said "Goodnight" to his children; they thanked him for buying Frank and said they had a fun day. He replied, "So did I."